FOR BLANCA

Isolation Journal, Vol 3

© 2021 Barb Reynolds

All rights reserved. This book, or any portion thereof, may not be reproduced or used in any manner without the expressed written permission of the publisher, except for the use of brief quotations in a book review.

print ISBN: 978-1-09836-387-1

VOLUME THREE

ISOLATION
JOURNAL

BARB REYNOLDS

DAYS 242-243

1.

OH HAPPY DAY!!!
BIDEN & HARRIS WIN THE ELECTION
BY 4 MILLION VOTES!

I danced all day! I laughed, I cried, I danced some more! I watched people dancing on TV from all over the country —even in other countries! Some people sang The Wicked Witch is Dead! Some people torched MAGA hats. It was glorious. I felt hope for the first time in four years.

2.
One of my favorite parts of the election result coverage yesterday was when one of the newscasters said "Oh well, it doesn't matter what Trump is tweeting, he is irrelevant now."
YES!!!!!

3.
OXYMORON: A figure of speech which produces an incongruous, seemingly self-contradictory effect.

OXY: Sharp, keen, acute.
MORON: Trump

So, you see the contrast there.

4.
Blanca is so exhausted from all of our dancing that she is twitching in dreamland.

5.
Self-Assignment: Revise a poem you brought to your writing group.

> The breeze was just enough.
> We teased the edge, water licking
>
> & lapping, tide tugging. We dipped
> in & out, craving to be taken,
>
> fearing the depth of our undertow.
> Hot hands hungry, we dove in—
>
> thirsty & tumbling, greedy
> & fumbling. Our island flooded daily.

6.
COUNTDOWN:

73 DAYS until the Wackadoodle-in-Chief is GONE!!!

7.
He spied like a spy would spy if he were a spy.

8.
I can't walk Blanca in the neighborhood anymore, she's too vulnerable. There is a huge cat that actually stalks her! We were stopped at some grass and Blanca was going about her beeswax when the cat arched its back and started creeping toward her! I had to step in because Blanca no longer has peripheral vision and didn't see or hear the cat. And then there are the coyotes at dusk and dawn. So, I'm the watchdog now.

DAYS 244-245

1.
I think isolation has worn down my standards for humor—I crack up every time I see that commercial where a woman opens the overhead cabinet and eighteen thousand Rubbermaid containers fall on her head and knock her down. I wonder how many takes that took.

2.
They were jumpy as they jumped in their jumpers.
The junkie junked the junk in his trunk.
They mucked up mucking the muck.

3.
Democracy Now! HEADLINE:

"An Unprecedented Attack on Democracy": Trump Escalates Effort to Overturn Biden Election Victory

(Can you say Poor Loser?)

4.
Blanca, AKA *Little Beggy Begger from Beggyville, USA*, is begging.

5.
WRONG: PG&E is charging me a "high-usage fee" that they say is state-mandated. But really, during a pandemic? When people are supposed to stay home and will, of course, use more gas & electricity than usual?! That's just wrong to do to people.

6.
I have a question:
When dogs sleep, why do they smell like corn chips?

7.
Self-Assignment: Write a poem from your notebook.

> Prescient versus nescient, gender
> versus engender. Every time
> that phone rang she jumped.
>
> One foot planted in commitment,
> the other dangling in desire.
> Situated, grainy, sanguine, bereave.
>
> What's it like
> always looking at his back?

8.
I have a little issue with insomnia…so a friend gave me brownies made with wacky-tobacky! Yum and Zzzzz.

9.
What was I saying? Oh yeah: I'm binge-watching The Queen's Gambit on Netflix. Three friends told me about it and it's super good! So well done, perfectly cast, and it's nice to remember more than I thought I would about chess. Plus, you can't go wrong watching a clever woman defeat all the men!

DAYS 246-247

1.
Alex Trebek died. ☹

I used to be a *Jeopardy* freak. Everyone knew I wouldn't answer the phone between 7-7:30pm. I think it was my stress-reliever when I was an investigator. Anyway, about 15 years ago I got an email to try out, so I went to a hotel in San Francisco and sat in a ballroom with 150 other people. They gave us a sheet of paper with 50 blanks, then they flashed question after question from any category onto a big screen and you had six seconds to jot down your answer. Suffice to say, it is much easier playing at home on the couch! It was hard! Only 8 out of our 150 went on to the next round. I didn't care— it was an exhilarating experience, and I smiled for days after for just having done it.

Thanks for everything, Alex.

2.
Self-Assignment: Write a poem from your notebook.

> Flotsam & jetsam,
> consortium, complete.
> The doorbell rings,
> saving us from ourselves.
>
> She didn't warn me
> but I knew
> I'd rather be alone
> than to be put down
> & squeezed dry
>
> by someone who is supposed
> to love & honor & cherish me.
> Robins sing their last songs;
> light of the moon, a beacon.
>
> At six I knew.

3.
FUNNY!

My friend Ken sent me this joke that's going around:

A Catholic, a woman of color, a teacher, and a Jew walk into the White House, along with a rescue dog.... That's it! No joke!

(Yay! Our Saviors!)

4.
Can we just talk about those BLOOPERS?? hee hee hee

a) FOUR SEASONS SNAFU !!!!! The Repubs meant to book a big press conference at the swanky Four Seasons Hotel and instead it was booked at Four Seasons Total Landscaping!!! Rudy Giuliani et al. had to give their speeches in the nursery's parking lot!!! LMFAO

b) YOSEMITE!!! Not only does our leader not know that Kansas City isn't in Kansas, but he has no idea how to pronounce Yosemite! We should be so proud.

5.
Blanca is the Cutiest Cutie Pie from Cutieville, USA.

6.
What a little comma can do:

Let's eat, Grandma!
Let's eat Grandma!
:-)

DAYS 248-249

1.
Democracy Now! HEADLINE:

Can Trump Pardon Himself? Trump's Desperate Bid to Stay in Power & Avoid Prosecution

The Tyrant wants to pardon himself! I think the fussy baby needs a bottle & a blankie.

2.
Hands down.
Hit the shower.
No skin off my nose.

3.
Democracy Now! HEADLINE:

Give ME the Pardon!
Ronnie Long, Free After 44 Years, Demands Justice for His Wrongful Conviction

(Moron-in-Chief, this is the proper use of a pardon)

4.
Self-Assignment: Write a poem from your notebook.

> In the long hours of my heated insomnia,
> you travel the circumference of my heart.
> Dominant versus recessive, shadow
>
> versus light. The energy that denying it requires.
> Intrepid, conceive, endear, Valhalla. An offering,
> to replace what she couldn't give.

5.
Covid numbers rise, hospital beds & morgues are filling up. People continue to gather, without masks, contract & spread Covid. I feel like I'll be in my house forever.

6.
There is a book called *The Gift of Fear*, by Gavin DeBecker (1997). The year it came out, I gave it as Christmas presents. What I love about the author's message is: pay attention to your intuition—it's there for a reason.

Especially women. We are socialized to be nice. For example, a woman comes home with bags of groceries and a strange man offers to help her carry them to her door. She says *No, thanks*, but he pushes and insists. The hair on the back of her neck stands up, but, not wanting to be *rude*, she ignores those instincts and acquiesces.
It doesn't end well for the woman.

It's OK to say to say *Thank you, no*— for no other reason than you are not comfortable. No explanation required.

7
Self-Assignment: Write a poem from lines in your notebook.

> Hyperbole, mimic, Folie à deux.
> Hanging versus pregnant chads.
> They needed a shaded getaway
>
> from the burning of their days.
> The sun descends, at first slowly.
> Later, driving around, killing
>
> time, he turned up the car radio
> louder than I knew it could go.
> Atheist, shame bombs, flaming
>
> blamer. *Quick! Hang a left*
> *down the back alley of Adventure,*
> *where we rarely go.*

DAYS 250-251

1.
She confided her confidence confidentially in the confidante.
He competently competed with the completely incompetent.

2.
Beat a dead horse.
We can do better. How about:
belabor the subject,
go on & on,
pound my point into the ground?

3.
Blanca isn't eating today. She has digestive issues and takes half an antacid nightly, which usually does the trick—but every couple of weeks her tummy gurgles & wrenches and she doesn't want to eat. She just wants to lie in her window and sleep. I used to be able to coax her with a scrambled egg or rice or cottage cheese around 10am, but not now. She should be hungry by dinner.

4.
Rachel Maddow made a plea for people to stay home & stop spreading the virus. Suck it up and don't gather for Thanksgiving this year! If you must go to work, that's one thing, but stop any other kinds of gatherings! Stay home! Hospitals are full, there will be no room for you if you get sick. Numbers are spiking exponentially, worse than the first wave. Why aren't people making the connection?

I simply do not understand people who still insist on not wearing masks. I had two Fed Ex guys come to my door last week with no masks on.

5.
I know — no one's going to show me everything
We all come and go unknown
Each so deep and superficial
Between the forceps and the stone

~Joni Mitchell, *Hejira*

6.
I think Joni Mitchell is <u>the</u> most brilliant lyricist. I got to meet her once! Eve is an architect and she got some swanky invitations to a private art opening of Joni's own paintings! I happened to be standing at the door from where she emerged to greet guests, and as she came along saying hello and shaking hands, we held hands and looked into each other's eyes for what felt like ten minutes but was probably three whole seconds. All I could muster was, "Hi Joni" – and smile, smile, smile.

7.
Rachel Maddow HEADLINE:

Healthcare Workers on Front Lines Feel They're Fighting Losing Battle as Public Flouts Safety Rules.

8.
NY Times HEADLINE:

Airports See Rise in Travelers as Officials Warn of Deadly Consequences. Health experts asked Americans to stay home over Thanksgiving, but up to 50 million people could be traveling over the holiday.

Who the what???!!!

DAYS 252-254

1.
Self-Assignment: Write a poem from your notebook.

> He kissed me on the cheek
> eight or nine times quickly,
> like a machine gun, an ambush.
>
> Earmark, cylinder, accurate, deplete.
> It would have been treachery
> to let him in. False logic,
>
> impossible passion. The shutdown
> order goes into effect
> at midnight.

2.
Donald Jr. has COVID.
I'm sure he'll get the super drugs no one else but The Fascist-in-Chief's family is getting.

3.
NY Times HEADLINE:

G.O.P. Officials Face Choice Between Will of Voters and Will of a President Falsely Claiming Fraud

4.
Question asked, question answered.

5.
I have very long arms, in contrast to Eve's... short ones. I have to buy my shirts in the next size up just so the sleeves will fit. She calls me Orangutan. I call her Pterodactyl.

6.
Self-Assignment: Write a poem from your notebook.

>	We share the same cadence
>	& torso, a way of glancing
>
>	without really looking.
>	I got that from her. Blank
>
>	notebook, blue gel pen, Fuji
>	apple. A nest made of needles
>
>	and dead flowers to fall into.
>	Err on the side of kindness.
>
>	On the other side of revenge
>	is forgiveness.

7.
I just learned the best way to store basil is to stand it up in a vase of water, like cut flowers. And the best way to save avocados is to let them ripen on the counter, then put them in the fridge.

8.
Heard it through the grapevine.

DAYS 255-256

1.
I have a question:

Isn't the person who says, *Love the sinner, hate the sin,* sinning?

2.
Watched *The Glorias* on Amazon Prime. Fantastic movie about Gloria Steinem, based on her book *My Life on the Road*, and directed by Julie Taymor.

SO WELL DONE. I love this quote from the movie:
"If men could get pregnant, abortion would be a sacrament!"

3.
The Glorias reminded me of my teenaged years (~15-17½) when Eve & I were involved in the women's movement after school and on weekends. We rallied for the ERA, painted signs, even wrote a monthly column in the N.O.W. Times called "Age of the Young Feminists." One weekend in 1979, we told mom we were going to stay at a friend's, but instead we jumped into a van with four other women and drove up to San Francisco to march in the Pride parade as part of the N.O.W. contingency!

4.
Somehow my friends in high school found out I was gay and outed me in the most betraying & ostracizing way. It was, as they say, a very *formative experience*. It took forty years to be able to write about it, and I published *Poem That Took 40 Years (Part One)* in Stonewall's Legacy Anthology (2019).

5.
All three parts are on my website, but here is Part One:
POEM THAT TOOK 40 YEARS

I don't know how long I held
that receiver, curly cord
anchoring me in a thick fog
of stun. *Details swirl and cloud.*

It was one night in eleventh grade.
My mom called out that the phone
was for me. I ran to the kitchen, Hello?

LEZ!!!   Click.
I said to myself—or perhaps out loud—
Oh my God, that was Mina. Mina,
my best friend. She stashed
her brace for scoliosis in my room
every morning on her way to school,
we smoked my mom's cigarettes, hated
the world together.

The next morning, standing at my locker,
wondering how she found out,
I felt eyes burning my face, my back.
Friends ignored, or stared
until I looked away. In the bathroom,
I saw my name on the stall wall
in black letters—or were they red—
Barb Reynolds is a *LEZ*.

I washed my hands, breathed air
into the folds of my lungs,
and began the long walk
through the halls. I perfected
a shell. And it encased me.

DAYS 257-258

1.
NY Times HEADLINE:

President Trump Authorizes Government to Begin Transition to President-Elect Biden's Administration

It's about friggin' time!

2.
In toto
Et al.
Ad Nauseum

3.
Self-Assignment: Write a poem from your notebook.

> We live in arrears, spending
> the second half of our lives
> dissecting the first. Bridge,
> moat, chasm, alight.
> When my mother was dying
> she swore she saw Marilyn Monroe
> in a bright, beautiful garden.
> I'm pretty sure it was the morphine,
> but I'll never really know.

4.
I have a question:

If smelling burnt toast is sign of a stroke, what does it mean when I smell sour milk out of nowhere?

5.
Watched Rachel. Ugh. So, the transition is finally happening, even though Trump still insists he'll fight the results, but in the meantime, he is wreaking havoc during his Lame Duck period (don't get me started on how stupid I think the Lame Duck thing is).

He has now pulled the U.S. out of the Open Skies Treaty,
he's destroying observer planes. Can you say Impulsive? Myopic?
Saboteur? Russian spy???

6.
Walking in Berkeley at night, after dragging my sister to a poetry
reading and then leaving at intermission—our compromise—
I tripped on a raised square of sidewalk. When I looked back at it
accusingly, I saw the words *NOTHIN'S WRONG* carved into the
concrete.

The next morning, going into surgery, I visualized a small growth,
nothing complicated, and those words. As they numbed the area,
I tapped my finger to distract myself from the pain of the needle and
I imagined the tumor untethered, rootless.

As the surgeon worked, I felt her hands moving against my temple
but could not feel the cutting itself. I thought about the vastness
of heart, the expansiveness of mind that one must have to write those
words: *Nothin's Wrong.* Everything's right. Then I felt it, and I became
it. And the cancer was simple.

7.
Started dipping a little yesterday, in anticipation of spending
Thanksgiving alone. Thanksgiving is my favorite holiday. No gifts,
just gathering with people you love around a big table, remembering
those who aren't here anymore, great food, giving thanks. For two
decades I hosted a day-after-Thanksgiving dinner for twenty of
my closest friends.

I'm thankful for all of the kindhearted people in the world. I'm
thankful for Blanca, for my true friends & loving family, and for Tina
& Tony J., who will be dropping off a yummy Thanksgiving plate **:-)**

DAYS 259-260

1.
Self-Assignment: Write a poem from your notebook.

> The smoke rises & drifts,
> dances & lingers, then separates
> into the air like lovers,
>
> knowing their heat will destroy them.
> Synesthesia, susurration,
> smile-messengers.
>
> Dry grass & dirt, like hay
> ground into clay, kick up as I feign
> walking. I arrive at the gate
>
> and take the last in-between seat
> people try to block with their stuff.
> Northern Flicker, Dark-Eyed
>
> Junco, Red Tailed Hawk. Breezes
> that linger. They take me back
> to you. Always to you.

2.
The sailor sailed the sailboat with the sails he got on sale.

3.
COUNTDOWN:

55 DAYS!!! Woot Woot!!! I'd usually say, "We could survive anything for 55 days," but with the Spy-in-Chief, I don't know…

4.
Still hating that so many people are traveling this holiday weekend, getting sick and spreading it around when they get home…

I loved seeing this:

TRAVEL PLANS THIS WEEKEND:
TO THE WINDOW, TO THE WALL,
THEN I MIGHT GO DOWN THE HALL

5.
Went to see what Blanca was barking at and it was a leaf. Started to sweep out back but it got too cold. Started to break down boxes in the garage but it got too cold. This winterlike fall is different.

6.
The carbineer combined the carbines with the carbides in the cabinet. The napper napped in the nape of Napata.

7.
s/wept
b/lock
c/lick

8.
I fell asleep to Dateline: Secrets Uncovered and woke up at 3am to that preacher guy with the goatee who looks like the devil and constantly asks for money.

DAYS 261-262

1.
Happy Thanksgiving! Woke up feeling really good, had my morning cuddles with Blanca, had a long chat with Eve over coffee, all is well. I'll make Blanca some rice and she'll get a little turkey. I'll make us a fire and we'll watch The Sound of Music. We'll sing along. OK, well, she'll sleep and I'll sing along, but anyway….

2.
While making our fire, that Breyer's commercial came on with Matilda the Cow and that little red-headed girl. I love that one. Next, a bunch of cats were dressed up like they were in a country band… Then more cats dressed as cowboys in a saloon. Oh brother. I like recording things so I can forward through commercials. I also like recording Rachel so I can decide when I'm ready to watch it.

3.
Roger
10-4
Copy that

4.
Self-Assignment: Throw a poem together from your notebook.

> Their bones might be picked clean, licked
> clean, locked away in a suffocating drawer
> of marble, clanging together
>
> like church bells—remnants, real, rummage,
> reveal—but I'm the skeleton rattling around
> in the remains of my life.

5.
Graduated from an IPhone 6s to an 11. It came with a 2x2 info card in .0004 font and I had to literally get my magnifying glass to read it. After all that, the tiny writing tells me to go to their website for info...

6.
I may or may not have had 10½ tater tots with my healthy salad last night.

7.
At a spa in Sedona, on the menu between *Massage* and *Facial*, was *Past Life Regression* and when I went under, I saw myself as Jim —in a tweed suit and scuffed brown shoes. It was 1885, and I was Jim. It was me in that buckboard, guiding my horses home to the cabin I built, where my wife died in childbirth. I saw the whole thing, tears rolling into my ears as I lay on the table, incense wafting.

8.
A few years before the Sedona experience, a shaman told me that in my last life, between Jim & now, I was a woman who ran an orphanage. Then she looked up from her gongs & feathers and said, I rarely do this, but I need to tell you: *You can only do so much for the kids.*

9.
Got a small grocery delivery. The packer packed the eggs at the bottom of the box and four were smashed to smithereens, the half & half had two days before expiring, and the meat was lukewarm. Still, I am grateful for the help!

DAYS 263-264

1.
NY Times HEADLINE:

NYC Will Reopen Elementary Schools in Response to Criticism that Activities Like Indoor Dining are Taking Priority Over Well-Being of Children.

2.
Is it just me, or do you agree this is not a good reason to open elementary schools? Seems to me, they should shut down indoor dining while we are spiking, not <u>also</u> open elementary schools!

3.
Off the cuff
On the money

4.
Self-Assignment: Throw a poem together from your notebook.

> It may look like a tango at first: arms joined
> at the hands, pointing toward some future together,
>
> then reversing just as strong. Capacious, busted,
> selfie, unite. I was minding my own business,
>
> minding no one. I was with you in a warm bath,
> in a hotel room with no view.

5.
I don't understand people who say the Holocaust didn't happen.

6.
Sometimes when I cannot sleep and can no longer lie there trying,
I watch from the front window as deer stroll yard to yard, searching.
The drought has taken their sustenance, the developing, their habitat.
I leave apples & carrots—apologies for the greed of my species.

7.
The titillating tidbit tore through the tiny town.

8.
Democracy Now! HEADLINES:

The Lame-Duck Executioner: Trump Prepares to Execute Five Prisoners in Closing Days of Presidency.

Firing Squads, Poison Gas, Electric Chair: Trump Moves to Expand Ways to Kill Prisoners.

9.
I am infuriated at things Trump is doing in his lame duck period, wondering WHAT in the world is THE line that needs to be crossed exactly before someone, anyone, says, *OK buddy, let's go*, and hauls his ass out of there?? If THIS isn't the time, I don't know what is.

It's like telling a kid they'll get in trouble if they do XYZ, but when they actually do XYZ, they're given an ice cream cone. Or, in this case, a cheeseburger.

DAYS 265-266

1.
Self-Assignment: Write a poem from your notebook.

Sitting
in the
window
at my
sister's
house
in the
LA hills,
83 steps
up from
the street.

Mourning
doves
have taken
shelter
in the eaves
over
the balcony.
Immense,
intense,
offense,
dispense.
She banged
a drum,
he blew
a horn.
Joy
ripped
a hole
in fear.

2.
I'm looking into an online Geography class. That's one subject I tuned out of in school and I've always wanted to be better at it.

3.
Rudy Giuliani is looking into how the Baby-in Chief can pardon him! I'd laugh if it wasn't so pitiful. Then, Jimmy Fallon says, "It's gotta be pretty bad when your own attorney says, *Hey dude, you gotta help me outta this.*" That made me laugh.

4.
This, on the other hand, did not make me laugh:

Gavin Newsom, our hip & beloved Governor, was seen eating at French Laundry in Napa with at least ten other people sitting close together and none of them were wearing masks! "*Embarrassed, Newsom apologizes…*" Tell it to the wall. Un-friggin-believable. SO SURPRISING, SO DISAPPOINTING!

5.
The groupies grouped into groups while eating grouper fish.

6.
There are certain companies that have horrible LGBTQ equality ratings—or, more to the point, they are actively using their proceeds to fund right-wing and anti-gay causes. For instance, I don't eat at Chic-fil-A, Carl's Jr, or Domino's Pizza. I won't be driving a Tesla, gassing-up at Exxon-Mobil, or shopping for clothes at Ross. Info at Corporate Equality Index 2020 from the Human Rights Campaign: https://assets2.hrc.org/files/assets/resources/CEI-2020.pdf

DAYS 267-268

1.
First time out today since dropping my ballot— I took Blanca to the vet for a nail trim. Each morning I let her outside, turn on the furnace, then get back under the covers. When she comes in, she walks around the entire house. It sounds like tap dancing on the wood floors. Then, after she's made sure I'll never fall back to sleep, she lies down on her bed under my bed for a nice nap before breakfast.

2.
Zero in on
For the birds

3.

PEER

PEEL

PEAL

APPEAL

APPEAR

APPAREL

PERIL

PEAR

PEAL

PEEL

Say that a couple times fast. 🙂

(I think Blanca just rolled her eyes.)

4.
I have questions:

Have you ever sung loudly when no one was around?
If so, for how long? And, what made you stop?

5.
Yesterday it was warm enough to be outside so I planted my winter garden greens. It felt so good to be out there. Blanca found a warm spot on the cement and kept me company. We are under a strict Stay at Home order for the next month, so I've had to cancel visits here again. Ugh.

6.
Simulating the test, he simultaneously caused the simul.

7.
I happened to look out my front window just as a workman across the street put his ladder on this rack on the side of his truck and then cranked something that hoisted it onto the top & secured it. I said *So that's how they do that*! For someone who usually looks over as I'm driving in time to see roadkill, that's quite an improvement!

8.
Good grief
Skin in the game

9.
Rudy, Rudy, Rudy.
Don't you know not to fart near an open mic??
I think the woman next to you got whiplash when it happened. SNL did a great spoof on it so we can relive that stinkin' moment ad nauseum. (See what I did there?)

10.
He flatly flattened to flat with his flatulence. Ew.

DAYS 269-270

1.
COUNTDOWN:

46 more days!! Woo Hooooooooo!

2.
Self-Assignment: Write a poem with lines from your notebook.

> I remember aftershocks
> and peering out through fissures.
> Harbinger versus portend,
> saccharine versus sugar.
> Even bricks and cement
> can only hold up for so long.
>
> I'm jumping off this crazy train,
> not even waiting for the next station.
> Mojo, starburst, gibbon, harbor.
> I knew it was freedom: not the kind
> someone else gives you,
> but the kind you give yourself.

3.
You'll be happy to know, I've started putting my clothes away again. (But I still haven't streamed Hamilton.)

4.
Trump isn't allowing the new Dept. of Defense people to share any incoming intelligence with the Biden/Harris team. He must really detest the United States.

5.
Criminy
Malarky
For crying out loud

6.
Tell me a story!

And she's like… and he goes… and she went… and he's all…

Don't tell me a story!

7.
He single-handedly singled out the singles.

8.
Let's talk about rejection letters. When you first start sending your stuff out you must be prepared for LOTS of rejections. A few years ago, my therapist and I decided to replace the word *rejection* with something less charged. So, I chose *sesame seed*. Now when I say, *I got a sesame seed today*, I almost giggle— and move on.

9.
Do-se-do yer partner… E-I-E-I-O

DAYS 271-272

1.
Self-Assignment: Write a poem from your notebook.

> Evening fell as quickly as the sun rose.
> Keel, karma, kilter, keck.
>
> I might be moving slowly,
> but I'm not cold yet. I surrender,
>
> go under, wade into the deepest
> marshes to find you. Even if I erase it all,
>
> even if I never do.

2.
Astray/ A stray
Dress/Redress
Semblance/Resemblance

3.
NY Times HEADLINE:

After the Students Came Back, Deaths Rose in College Town.

(ya think?)

4.
I have two long-time friends, Nancy M. and Tina G., and we're called *The Trio*. Tina's stepmother died of COVID yesterday on a vent in ICU, and Nancy's nephew died suddenly this morning of non-COVID related cardiac arrest. It is agonizing for people not to be able to be with their loved ones at these times.

5.
After almost ten months of isolation & not knowing how much longer, I remember Viktor Frankl. Frankl was an Austrian psychiatrist & neurologist, and a prisoner in concentration camps. With the exception of one sister, his entire family, including his wife, perished in the camps or ovens. Each day he watched fellow prisoners going mad around him, turning against each other, committing suicide, disappearing.

Frankl was the founder of Logotherapy, literally "healing through meaning," and this is how he survived. I hold a certificate in Logotherapy from graduate school. Frankl believed that one's search for meaning is the central motivating force in human beings, with three main tenets: *Everything can be taken from a man but one thing: the last of the human freedoms—to choose one's attitude in any given set of circumstances, to choose one's own way. When we are no longer able to change a situation, we are challenged to change ourselves. Between stimulus and response there is a space. In that space is our power to choose our response. In our response lies our growth and our freedom.*

Excellent book: *Man's Search for Meaning*, by Viktor E. Frankl

6.
Pushy, she pushed push-pins, then pushed people into pushing pencils.

Periodically, the period would be the end. Period.

People peopled the people-mover while other people peopled the peep-show ones at these times.

DAYS 273-274

1.
Democracy Now! HEADLINE:

Black Mom Swarmed & Beaten by Philly Riot Police with Toddler in Car Demands Officers Be Fired.

2.
Self-Assignment: Write a poem using lines from your notebook.

>Brittle with unturned yearnings
>and overdue blooms, bitter
>and sinewy from hard years
>
>of planting by hand. It makes sense,
>it's even wise at first. Doom-scrolling,
>gnawing, fair-weather friend.
>
>I wish you were here now. I wish
>I never opened the back door
>when you came knocking.

3.
I'm having the darnedest time finding this one piece to the jigsaw! I'm pretty sure Blanca hid it.

4.
Watching Dateline. Someone was killed and no one would testify except this 11-year-old girl! All of the adults hid. You go, girl. I can't wait to see what you do in life.

5.
NY Times HEADLINES:

U.S. Virus Death Toll Crosses 300,000 as Vaccinations Begin

Should Companies Require Employees to Take the Vaccine?

6.
He tossed his cookies.
She lost her head.

7.

Self-Assignment: Write a poem using lines from your notebook.

> The walls I'd built
> so carefully, last time
> I decided love wasn't for me,
> seem to be failing.
> You showed up
> and there I was,
> sweeping the mess.
> Phalange, grapefruit,
> tryptophan slumber.
> How so much of the world
> was in their clumsy
> and dangerous hands.

8.

I just watched a news story about a restaurant owner who is getting fined $1000/day for staying open & serving food when we are on a state-wide lockdown. He is doing this so he can pay his 30 employees. But, what is the cost of the lives lost in this process? I couldn't believe my eyes: how many people were dining there, maskless. Only the servers wore masks in this news clip. I think all of the diners should be fined as well.

DAYS 275-276

1.
NY Times reports that Trump was going to let White House staffers jump ahead and get the vaccine before anyone else. When this scheme was discovered, they backed off and said, *OK, well not <u>everyone</u> will jump ahead…* (but some will.)

Not surprising at all, but sickening nonetheless.

2.
COUNTDOWN: 37 DAYS!!!

3.
Biden & Harris are formally elected by the Electoral College to become the next President and Vice President of the United States! Trump keeps fighting the results.

4.
Self-Assignment: Write a poem using lines from your notebook.

> I crawl out through the windshield
> and point my beam down. Too much ash
> has built up, it chokes me, obstructs
> my view, makes me take the wrong
> damn turn every time.
>
> Shiplap versus beadboard, tongue
> & groove. I dropped anchor,
> you sailed away. How many waves
> have washed over us since then.
> How many have salted old wounds.

5.
Turns out I love the mystery jigsaw! Ordered another. Had more firewood delivered & stacked. Planted and trimmed. Broke another wine glass as I was putting it away. I buy two sets of plates and glasses at a time because I break so many.

6.
I am tiring of headlines, what the Attention-Seeker-in-Chief has done now during Lame Duck. Fowling things up, I guess...
(see what I did there?)

7.
OK, here's a headline that makes me happy:

BARR RESIGNS!

8.
Put all your eggs in one basket.
Red Letter Day.

9.
I have questions:

Did love ever line your heart with feathers?
Did you ever take your helmet off when your mom wasn't looking and ride free?

10.
Mistakenly, he mistook the mistake for a mistake.

DAYS 277-278

1.
This poem, which I first heard at the age of 16, keeps going through my mind: Pat Parker, the black lesbian feminist activist, wrote:

"For Straight Folks Who Don't Mind Gays, But Wish They Weren't So Blatant"

You know some people got a lot of nerve.
Sometimes, I don't believe the things I see and hear.

Have you met the woman who's shocked by 2 women kissing,
& in the same breath tells you that she's pregnant?
BUT GAYS SHOULDN'T BE BLATANT.

Or the straight couple sits next to you in a movie
& you can't hear the dialogue, cause of the sound effects.
BUT GAYS SHOULDN'T BE BLATANT.

And the woman in your office, spends your entire lunch hour
talking about her new bikini drawers & how much her husband likes them.
BUT GAYS SHOULDN'T BE BLATANT.

Or the "hip" chick in your class rattling a mile a minute --
while you're trying to get stoned in the john—
about the camping trip she took with her musician boyfriend.
BUT GAYS SHOULDN'T BE BLATANT.

You go in a public bathroom and all over the walls
there's John loves Mary, Janice digs Richard, Pépé loves Delores...
BUT GAYS SHOULDN'T BE BLATANT.

Or you go to an amusement park & there's the tunnel of love
& pictures of straights painted on the front & grinning couples
coming in and out.
BUT GAYS SHOULDN'T BE BLATANT.

Fact is, blatant heterosexuals are all over the place. Supermarkets, movies, on your job, in church, in books, on television every day and night, every place --even in gay bars—& they want gay men & women to go hide in the closet.

So to you straight folks I say: Sure, I'll go, if you go too, but I'm polite— so, after you.

2.
Cuddled with Blanca & a fire and *The Sound of Music* came on TV (again). Cracked up when the Captain says to Maria about her clothes:

C: You'll need a new dress
M: I don't have another one. When we entered the abbey, we gave up all worldly possessions & gave them to the poor.
C: What about [the one you're wearing]?
M: The poor didn't want this one…

Then I watched *The Last Holiday* with Queen Latifah. Burst out laughing at the part where she's getting a massage at a resort in Prague, and the masseuse starts flogging her with a branch as part of the treatment, but Queen doesn't understand so she grabs the branch and starts hitting the masseuse with it. Felt good to laugh. As Joni Mitchell says, *Laughing and crying,* it's the same release…

3.
Speaking of Queen, my ex-wife and I used to call Blanca *Queen La-Teefers* because of her severe underbite.

4.
Democracy Now! HEADLINE:

Shut It Down: Calls Grow to Close Fort Hood After Probe into Murders & Sexual Assaults at Army Base

Sexual assaults at an army base.

One soldier sexually assaulting a fellow soldier.

What about the very oath a soldier vows to uphold: to protect & support their fellow soldiers? Disgraceful. They should call it *Fort Trump.*

Some days I feel like we live in a world where there is very little decency left. I need to be exposed to & reminded of all of the positive and kind things people are doing, to balance it out.

5.
As I was coughing this morning I said to Eve:

When she coughs, do they call her Anne Hackaway??

OK, I thought that was pretty funny!
Eve said It's early, you're just warming up.
:-/

I told her if she had thought of it, she'd think it was hysterical.

6.
For Pete's sake!

Who is Pete? And why are we doing things for his sake??

7.
Self-Assignment: Write a poem using lines from your notebook.

The sun shined warm
on my morning shoulders,
the light clicked off
down the hall. Buzzards

versus hawks, compromise
versus giving in. I'm trying
to steer this train in smoothly,
rather than it squealing,

harsh & acrid, into the station.
I've become half-blind
and everything is covered
in soot—fallout from flames

ignited then doused, lit
and then smothered.
It was a dream I kept having,
and I'd wake up gasping.

DAYS 279-280

1.
Self-Assignment: Write a poem from your notebook.

>I lie on the cold, paper-lined
>exam table, wishing there was
>a nice Van Gogh
>
>up on the peeling ceiling.
>Cyclopes, Merfolk, Unicorns, Phoenix.
>She kissed me on the mouth
>
>like an exclamation point.
>I asked too many questions.
>She kept it all to herself.

2.
You know it's bad when you find yourself singing along to commercial jingles (and really getting into it)

3.
Democracy Now! HEADLINES:

CIA-Backed Afghan Death Squads Massacred Children Inside Religious Schools in Campaign of Terror

As Wealthy Countries Hoard Vaccine Supply, Pandemic Could Rage in Poor Countries Until 2024

Evictions Are Violence: Millions Could Lose Homes Amid COVID Pandemic if Federal Moratorium Expires

4.
Sump Pump
Lump Rump
Frump Chump
Dump Trump

5.
Self-Assignment: Write a poem from your notebook.

You kissed me so right, the kiwi in my hand almost peeled itself
            the birds in my trees held their breath
            the tide broke free from the moon
            the

(Oh forget it. Start over)

THINK
She was asking for it.

You think you know what it's like
until he's on you with a knife
and the other one's standing by.
Think. Would anyone ever really
ask for that?

Just get rid of it.

You think it's no big deal
until you've had to experience it,
or until a man in a suit with a flag pin
says you can't have one.

Man, I'm starving!

You think you know what hunger is
until the first time your stomach burns,
and you realize that's just the beginning
of not enough.

DAYS 281-282

1.
Had quite the harrowing day.

The cyst on Blanca's leg turned out to be a tumor and it ruptured. I was able to stop the bleeding and took her to the vet, who has been my vet for 25 years. The tumor happened to be connected to an artery and emergency surgery was performed. I drove around crying, and then thought it's probably not a good idea to be driving— so, after getting gas, I came home.

2.
Sat down to write and had no concentration. Broke down some boxes, swept outside. Mopped the floors, where Blanca's blood had left a trail. I think I prayed. Spoke with friends, zoned out.

3.
I was told to call the vet at 4, so when my phone rang at 2pm and it was them, my stomach dropped. Bracing myself for the worst, they were calling to say surgery went well and Blanca was eager to come home :-)

Dr. Maureen Dorsey is the hero of the universe! Thank you, Thank you, Thank you for saving my little girl today! My heartfelt thanks also to Jana, Emma, Megan, Anna, Lupé, and Dr. Cecilie Hart. Oakland Veterinary Hospital rocks!

4.
With a cone on her head and a long row of sutures near her rear, Blanca was bummed to have a bum bum. :-/

5.
Zero sleep last night. Stoned out of her mind (no, I'm not talking about myself in the third person) and in lots of pain, Blanca literally jumped up every 10-15 minutes and I'd soothe her back to sleep. She was completely disoriented with the cone on her head, so I kept a little light on so she could see when she woke up through the night. Second night was a little better.

6.
I am hearing about a mutation of the Coronavirus that makes it even easier to contract. That just freaks me out. I absolutely cannot handle that right now.

7.
Blanca's come through the worst of the pain & discomfort from surgery. The drugs have helped a lot. I asked Dr. Hart to increase the pain meds over the weekend, and that was just the relief Blanca needed. She is such a trooper. I was told, when I brought her home, not to let her scoot— whatever I do. Scooting could pull the sutures apart and she'd have to be re-stitched and risk infection. Not on my watch!

8.
Eve sent me a YouTube video of a DIY e-collar made from twine and cut-up pieces of a foam pool noodle! You make a necklace that allows her more vision and movement, while still blocking access to the sutured area. I happen to have a pool, so I went in search of a noodle and found a purple one in the bin! It took about five minutes to make, and she looks mahhhhvelous in it!
So far, it's 100% effective.

9.
HUGE THANKS to Alison & Lee for bringing me flowers when I was a wreck during Blanca's surgery, to Shannon for picking up Blanca's pain meds & dropping them off, and to Dean for watching Blanca in the backyard so I could take a shower!!

DAYS 283-284

1.
Well, if Dr. Dorsey is the hero of this story, then cancer certainly is the villain.

Dr. Hart left a voicemail that the pathology report came back as cancer. I blanked out through the rest of her message, but I do remember the part about learning more when I speak with Dr. Dorsey on Monday.

2.
She calmed the calmless during the clammy calamity.

3.
I sure cried my little eyes out when Dr. Hart's message hit me.
The idea of looking over and Blanca not being there…
my grief is bottomless, just at the thought of it.

4.
Dean and I were talking about the Christmas and Mother's Day presents we made as little kids in Elementary school. He remembered the multi-colored plastic lanyards, and I told him that in Emergency Response, if I saw a worker wearing their badge on a lanyard around their neck, I'd say to myself, *You might as well show up to a call and say, 'Hi, my name is Choke-Me-Now!'*

5.
I like that we've done away more & more with "feminine endings" on words—like Actress, Stewardess, Directrice, Benefactress, Comedienne, and my personal favorite, Executrix. Funny: when I looked it up, there was this reference: *Seductress (see Dominatrix)*

6.
Monday morning. Called Dr. Dorsey ten minutes after they opened. I was surprised at how much my hands were shaking when I dialed. Anna said that the doctor was just handed the file, so she will look everything over and give me a call back sometime today between patients.

7.
Why is it that when you are aware of time,
like waiting for this phone call,
it d r a g s   on   soooo   slo-o-o-owly ?

7.1

7.2

7.3

7.4

7.5

7.6

7.7

7.8

7.9

8.
She waited impatiently for the patient to be patient.

9.
Dr. Dorsey called. She said they did not get clean margins, for a number of reasons that made a lot of sense to me, but the soft-tissue sarcoma has not metastasized. The tumor grew into the muscle in the leg/hip, so she had to remove some muscle. No treatment suggested at this time, just let her leg heal.

10.
COUNTDOWN: 29 Friggin' Days!!!!

DAYS 285-287

1.
Blanca graduated out of her pool-noodle necklace. For the first time in a week she slept free! We could cuddle and she could nuzzle, she could lie in her window and lick her paws after breakfast, her favorite. She only tried to scoot once this morning and I had to yell her name (she's hard-of-hearing) and she stopped immediately.

2.
Blanca's the troopiest trooper from Trooperville, U.S.A.

3.
I was thinking about mass production versus the small farmer, which lead me to think about how many people there are in the world, and that lead me to wondering if China still has that law limiting each couple to having just one child. According to Wikipedia, *in 2013 the National Health and Family Planning Commission relaxed the one-child restriction, allowing couples to have two children, IF one parent, rather than both parents, was an only child.* What the who??

Then in 2016 that rule was abolished, allowing all couples to have two children, because they now have too many men, too many old people, and too few young people.

I've had the discussion with friends & colleagues before: How many kids should someone responsibly have? I believe a couple should figure out how many kids they could fully care for *if they were on their own*—in case something should happen to the other parent and they had to do it alone—and then do that.

4.
You're putting me on!

5.
Eve's friends & I tried to roast her for her 50th birthday but she's so darn good, we had nothing. For her own birthday, Eve hired the "Do-Good Bus" and took twenty of her friends to volunteer at a soup kitchen! The worst thing I can say is that for most of my life she led me to believe that I have huge feet and hers are much smaller— just a few years ago I busted her--she wears the same size!

6.
If it's not one thing, it's your mother…

7.
You'll be happy to know that Blanca, AKA: *The Amazing Wonder Dog*, has not tried once to lick her incision. And now when she wants to scoot, she looks over at me and I shake my head *No*, and she gives it up. I'm pretty sure she's part human, just sayin'.

8.
She licked the habit of licking with her last lick.

9.
Self-Assignment: Write a poem from your notebook.

> I see a woman pushing a dirty baby stroller—garbage & cloth crammed
> inside its broken canopy, once painted brightly in primary colors
> but now faded and moving through the sea of downtown homeless,
>
> bags dangling from its sides like boat fenders.
> Incision, incisor, incinerate, insist. He banished me for a month,
> then invited me to return, to resume my place
>
> within the pitted and chipped walls of his palace,
> when he could no longer recall
> why I was gone.

DAYS 288-290

1.
NY Times HEADLINES:

Covid Virus Variant is called B.1.1.7.

That's all I can deal with today...

2.
Let's face it, the faces of the facing-off fascists need a facelift.

(In other words, *God don't like ugly*)

3.
Quality of life. That's what it comes down to. The hardest part of being a parent— I was going to say to an animal but it also applies to people— is knowing when to let them go.

I lie in bed and think about Blanca. I don't want her last months/years to be going through treatments, being on meds and in discomfort, wearing a cone on her head—or even her darling noodle necklace. That is no quality of life for her.

I say, let her be and when she becomes uncomfortable, stop her suffering. Easy to say, excruciating to execute.

4.
I was going to write about all of the horrendous pardoning the Traitor-in-Chief is doing but I am having a perfectly good day and want to keep it that way.

5.
Boob Tube
Love Boat
Hole-in-the-Wall Diner

6.
I love everything about *The Sound of Music,* except for the song *Sixteen Going on Seventeen* between Liesl and Rolf. I love their dance, but not the words: she starts off all empowered & frisky, then he says, "You're a baby, you need someone looking after you." So, she changes and says, "You're right, I'm naïve, I need someone looking after me." Deflating how we buy into these things.

I love the dances in *Singin' in the Rain,* but not how piggish and forceful Gene Kelly is with Debbie Reynolds! I hadn't remembered that part at all, but it was really a turn-off when I re-watched it a couple nights ago. I endured it to get to the songs & dances.

I remember liking *West Side Story* when I was a kid, but I watched it last year and I couldn't even endure it long enough to get to the dances —it was so racist!

I remember really liking *Oklahoma*! as a kid, but I better re-watch that one as well…
:-/

7.
I don't understand people that see how our president is behaving, like a whiny sore-loser on the playground, and still choose to support that. What kind of role model is he? How do you praise that kind of behavior, and then expect your own children to behave with dignity when they lose? Should it be a free-for-all now? No one has to respect another, no conceding when someone loses fair & square? The implications of where this is heading is frightening to me.

DAYS 291-293

1.
I have a question:

Is a prostitute a *layperson*?

2.
Righty-tighty, lefty-loosey.

3.
I was watching Rachel and there was a story: "Pentagon anxiety rises as officers wait for Trump's next unpredictable move......"
And I ask, *Wait? Why? Why are we just sitting here waiting for his next move instead of removing him?* I must say, this Trump occupancy has been eye-opening, and now that push has definitely come to shove, I dare say I am not impressed with our wimpy leaders.

4.
Self-Assignment: Write a poem from your notebook.

> Subrogation versus sublimation, threadbare
> versus worn. We all know we will die one day;
> it's out there as a fuzzy, intangible given.
>
> Consequences versus outcomes, infatuation
> versus true love. A family of three
> smoothly carved ducks sit on a shelf
>
> in another kid's room,
> at the end of their hallway
> on another street.

5.
COUNTDOWN: 3 WEEKS, 1 DAY, 9 HOURS, 41 MINUTES, 14 SECONDS

6.
"I do not wish women to have power over men, but over themselves."
~Mary Wollstonecraft

This quote came as a gift from my friend Nancy M., printed on a tea towel from radicalteatowel.com. This led me to look up Mary Wollstonecraft (1759-1797), and I learned that she was an English writer, philosopher, and advocate for women's rights. She was also the mother of Mary Shelley, who wrote *Frankenstein* and was married to Percy Shelley. Who knew?

7.
Just binged-watched the first three seasons of ATYPICAL on Netflix. I didn't want it to end! Turns out, there will be a 4th & final season released soon.

8.
THANKS to my SURROGATES

The whole It takes *a village* thing is true: I couldn't have come through my childhood as well as I did without surrogates along the way who helped me.

There was Mrs. Stannage in the elementary school office—she knew things were bad at home and she was very sweet to me. Mrs. Kirk was our housekeeper for a few years when Mom had to go back to work after the divorce, and she was like a grandmother. In Junior High and High School, Carol Berman, the mom of one of Eve's friends, gave me extra attention and called me *Songbirdie* because I'd sing for her. She knew I was different, knew Eve & I had it hard, and her love & support felt unconditional, like Uncle Gene's. She told me I could do or be anything.

Hey, even in *The Sound of Music*, Liesl would have kept pining over that stupid Rolf if Maria hadn't come along to offer guidance.

DAYS 294-296

1.
Democracy Now! HEADLINE:

Trump Plots to Overturn Election: An Attack on Democracy or a Scheme to Make Millions for Himself?

(Two guesses)

2.
They were moved to remove him so he couldn't make his next move.

3.
Blanca got her sutures out and she's doing great! Jana said not to bathe her for a few days—no wonder Blanca almost skipped to the car…

4.
It's New Year's Eve, and here's a good one:

2020 ends in two days.
We may have our differences,
but I think we can all agree:
What. The. Fuck. Was. That.

5.
I know things don't change the second both hands hit 12 tonight, but energetically we need the shift. A new year, a new president, a new America. We can never go back to what we were. Let's take what we've learned and move forward, with more kindness in our hearts for each other, for everything we have endured.

6.
I believe in the Oxford comma.

7.
I watched the Avoider-in-Chief on the news, tooling around in his golf cart while his own country is falling apart. I saw a sign on a telephone pole:

TRUMP DOESN'T CARE IF YOU LIVE OR DIE

and it's true. He doesn't even care about the people who keep donating to him. In the four hours it took him to play 18 holes of golf, 5000 people died of COVID in California alone.

8.
COUNTDOWN: 18 more disgusting days

9.
I feel like I'm crawling toward the finish line, grit under my nails.

10.
Self-Assignment: Write a poem from your notebook.

> Charcoal smudged, graphite
> pushed across the page. Pail
>
> versus bucket, resuscitation,
> borborygmi, throwing shade.
>
> My fingers drew her outline
> from shoulder to hip,
>
> accentuating her soft sides.

DAYS 297-298

1.
New Year's Day. Woke up early & showered, fed Blanca, made coffee, sat down at my desk & heard a loud noise— then all the power went out... Drove to the bottom of the hill to get reception and found out 127 homes are affected and it will be 4-5 hours before restoration. Let my sister & a friend know, drove back up the hill. Blanca slept through my absence, thankfully. Made a fire, 45 outside, 53 inside now. Made a bowl of cereal —or as Eve & I used to say as kids (and maybe last week), *Solabereal*. Blanca slept on her bed by the fire, completely knocked out. I sat in my brown leather swivel, feet up on the embroidered pouf, covered with a merino throw. Read some Naomi Shihab Nye, some Jericho Brown. Listened to Joni Mitchell's Archives: The Early Years and loved hearing her chat so much between songs, felt like I was there. Checked my email and got a *sesame seed*.

2.
I'm all ears

3.
Someone sent me an old black & white shot from the 40's/50's of a male boss interviewing a prospective female employee:

Man: We're looking for someone who can do the work of six men.
Woman: That's a shame, I was looking for a full-time job!

4.
She was correct to correct it correctly.
Certainly, I was certain of the uncertainty.

5.
I have a question:
Don't you sink if you *pull out all the stops*?

6.
Self-Assignment: Write a poem from your notebook.

>Silence
>rolls you over like a dog
>pins you under thumbs
>says *I don't care*
>says *Do what you will*

7.
When Blanca was younger and she saw an animal on TV, she would charge the TV, jump up with her paws on the big screen. If the animal ran out of frame, Blanca would race outside, thinking they ran out the back of the TV. It was hysterical.

8.
In/valid
Auto/immune
Anti/venom

9.
Did I mention I got a book to learn Origami? When I told Eve and Dean, they both laughed and asked if I was going to learn basket weaving also?
:-/
I'll show them—I'll make the best darn crane they've ever seen!

DAYS 299-300

1.
Democracy Now! HEADLINE:

"Find 11,780 Votes": Trump Pushes Georgia to Overturn Election in Move to Disenfranchise Millions

I listened to that 4-minute recording where Trump is bullying Georgia Secretary of State Brad Raffensperger into fraudulently fixing the election for him. Shameful, pathetic attempt. Now Fani Willis, District Attorney in Fulton County, GA, must decide if she will charge Trump for illegally trying to pressure Georgia officials to commit voter fraud.

2.
Geez, how much longer??
Let me look: 16 days until he's out of our misery!

3.
I was doing dishes, thinking about how laughter is contagious. I watched *Pretty Woman* yesterday for the first time in ten years, and the scene where Julia Roberts is lying on the floor cracking up watching *I Love Lucy* absolutely made me laugh out loud.

Then, while vacuuming, I thought about how just listening to another person laugh can make you laugh, makes a face involuntarily smile. Say, someone is telling you a funny story but they are laughing so hard just trying to get it out that soon everyone in the room is laughing, tears rolling down their faces—and they don't even know why! Isn't there some recording from the 60's or 70's of people laughing? I vaguely remember something like that from my childhood.

Then it hit me! America needs a Laughing Booth! It's like a photo booth but comfy & clean. Let's say, for 5 minutes you watch and listen to people from all over the world laughing. Imagine how you'd feel stepping out of that booth, how the rest of your day would go. Well, it made me smile just to think about it while I was dusting.

4.
At least there is a limit to what Trump is exempt from: The reason D.A. Fani Willis can charge Trump is because he is exempt from Federal crimes, not State crimes. As Senate Chairman Adam Schiff said about Trump: "He is without ethical compass."

5.
What a shot in the arm!
Just a dash
Club soda

6.
My friend Karen just sent me this funny:

Dear Bank of America,
I just want to find 11,780
more dollars in my savings
account. Everyone at your bank
counted wrong!

LOLOLOLOLOLOLOLOLOLOLOLOLOLOLOLOLOL

7.
If you're happy and you know it, clap your hands!

8.
Speaking of my friend Karen, we call each other *MF*. We partnered up in Emergency Response, going on calls together once a week for ten years. As you can imagine, most people weren't overjoyed to see us walking up to their doors, and we were called *MF* (not the abbreviated version) more times than we could count, so we started calling each other *MF*. We agreed that if our bosses heard us say that, we'd tell them it stood for *Sister Mary Frances*…

DAYS 301-302

1.
Mantra of the week: *We're all doing the best we can.*

A little voice in my head pops up in retort: *Not Trump! He could be doing so much better!* But, if he could he would. He is not capable of doing better, he is too far gone in his mental illness.

2.
Watched *Harold* and *Maude,* cooked meatballs, finished a round puzzle and started a square one. Paid bills. Changed a light bulb on the front porch, talked with a neighbor, walked around my backyard to see how the veggies are faring after heavy rains. Carried over more firewood. Made a fire and watched the documentary *Beyond Boundaries* on Amazon Prime, about Harvey Weinstein, the sexual predator. Very well done. And ick.

3.
I have a question:

Why do advertisers think it's a good idea to have loud pounding music in the background of commercials? It just makes me mute it and vow never to buy that product because their commercials are so obnoxious.

4.
Democracy Now! HEADLINE:

Ahead of Pro-Trump Protest, Proud Boys Leader Arrested for Burning BLM Banner at Black Church

OK, help me understand this: The Proud Boys is a white-nationalist violent fascist group. The leader of the Proud Boys is Enrique Tarrio. Enrique Tarrio is, himself, Afro-Cuban. An Afro-Cuban person burned the Black Lives Matter flag.

Is that internalized racism? Profound self-loathing? It's gotta go deep if he made it all the way up to Leader, just sayin'…

5.
None of the Republicans still backing Trump deserve to be re-elected. They have spit on their oaths.

6.
Time for more isolation funnies:

I haven't tried yoga, but I have tried bending over to pick up my keys, so I'm pretty sure I'd hate yoga.

Yesterday: Fixed my hair & makeup. Saw no one.
Today: Looked like Jack Nicholson from The Shining.
     Saw all of the people I know.
     All of them.

As I watched the dog chase her tail, I thought dogs are so easily amused. Then I realized I was watching the dog chase her tail.

You'd think I was wanted for murder, the way I jumped when there was a knock at my door.

7.
I was first drawn to this song by the music, then I heard these beautiful opening lyrics:

I couldn't utter my love when it counted
Ah, but I'm singing like a bird 'bout it now
I couldn't whisper when you needed it shouted
Ah, but I'm singing like a bird 'bout it now
                          ~Hozier, *Shrike*

8.
When I write I can only listen to classical/instrumental/ambient music, nothing with words. I've made a playlist of twelve different versions of Clair de Lune, another mix of incredible pianists Tammy Hall, Barbara Higbie, and Adrienne Torf. I love Dustin O'Halloran's piano solos, my favorite being Opus 23. Or Mischa Maisky's cello version of Ave Maria. Melts me.

For chores, it has to be upbeat, and my go-to right now is Katie Cash Band's *Gift Horse* album. When I'm cooking it's R&B, oldies, Sia, Joni. When friends are over and we're cooking together, we are also dancing—it is said, *If you haven't danced in Barb's kitchen, you haven't really been here…* ;-) Anyway, music is crucial.

9.
Crossing my fingers for Georgia tomorrow, and for our country.
XOXO

10.
Self-Assignment: Write a poem from your notebook:

> Amaryllis blooms paper-white
> in the cold morning sun. Kaleidoscope,
> regret, scrupulous, demure. The shine
>
> of his red tricycle caught my eye.
> Is it bad that I believe things people say
> when they make love to me?
>
> The last time you see her
> will be the last time
> you see her.

DAYS 303-306

1.
CAN YOU SAY *INSURRECTION & SEDITION??*

Well, holy crap, what a shit-show that was with the white-supremacist-Trump-mobster-thugs storming the Capitol! I watched the whole thing, yelling at my TV. (This is why I don't watch much news) That was the most unpatriotic display I have ever seen! Glad Congress went back to work, but how despicable that after all of the violence incited by Trump, 120 republicans still voted to oppose the electoral results. I shake my head and think to myself, those *repubs* are just horrible people to the core. And then I hope it's true, that karma *is* a bitch.

2.
And where in the world were all the police that should have been ready? There is something very wrong and suspicious there, indeed.

3.
In the meantime, **WE FLIPPED THE SENATE!!!!!** Let's not let all of this other drama distract from this history-making event! **STACEY ABRAMS, THANK YOU!!!**

4.
I turned on MSNBC for an update this morning and Nancy Pelosi is calling on Pence to invoke the 25th Amendment on the grounds that our tyrant president has gone completely wackadoodle and needs to be removed from power. I don't see Pence doing it—he's too meek/weak/oblique.

5.
I love that social media platforms are shutting Trump down. Jude sent me a funny from Ireland: Trump saying *"Follow me on Etch-a-Sketch"*

So friggin' funny.

6.
WICK
WHACK
WALK
WELK
WOKE

7.
She spoke when spoken to, as her spokes spoked down the street.
The burrier buried the barrier bar none.

8.
Nothing to sneeze at.

9.
GRACE: Elegance or beauty of form; a pleasing or attractive quality or endowment; favor or goodwill.

DISGRACE: The loss of respect, honor, or esteem; a person, act, or thing that causes shame, reproach, or dishonor; the state of being out of favor.

[insert picture of Trump here]

DAYS 307-310

1.
Are there enough adjectives in the English language to cover how I feel? Some days I don't know where to start.

2.
YAY! A person with scruples & a backbone!
Bill Belichick refuses to accept the Presidential Medal of Freedom from Trump!

3.
Self-Assignment: Write what you've done so far today.

Showered, fed Blanca. Compared sofa swatches that arrived in the mail, had the impeachment coverage on in the background but muted so I didn't have to listen to those repubs defending the Seditionist-in-Chief. Played with Blanca and her squeaky toy, signed a new book contract with Finishing Line Press for *Drawing Words*, out this summer. Called AAA to jump my car again, drove from Montclair to San Leandro & back. Decided I will start my car in the driveway & let it run for 20 minutes every other day, and on the other days I will drive it around.

4.
Look at all of the Democrat Senators testing positive for COVID after being forced to shelter during the mob siege with republicans who refused to wear masks! They should be expelled from the Senate and charged with attempted murder! One of the Democratic Senators is 75 and a breast cancer survivor! How dare you! Unforgivable.

5.
The republicans repugnantly show their repugnance repeatedly.

6.
Self-Assignment: Write a poem from your notebook.

>She dove from the pier, sleek
>& silhouetted, piercing
>
>still waters. Recalibration versus
>adjusting, weave versus
>
>swerve. She asked *Why
>are there Bibles in hotel rooms
>
>but not on airplanes?* I said,
>*Wild are animals not yet broken.*

7.
So, he sewed the sinewy sinew so-so.
She teared up when the tear tore.

8.
Democracy Now! HEADLINE:

Would You Patent the Sun? Polio Vaccine Inventor Jonas Salk's Son Urges More Access to COVID Vaccine

9.
We are just 7 days away from inaugurating Biden & Harris!

Trump is the only president in U.S. history to be impeached twice. Yet, he is somehow still allowed to grant pardons & order executions, withhold vaccines, on & on. He is poison.

DAYS 311-316

1.
The egret egressed through the ingress, ingressively.

2.
Played pool for the first time in a couple of months yesterday. I played solids against stripes, then practiced bank shots, slices, combos, long shots, rail shots. Weakest shot today: Long shots. Strongest: Combos & slices. I made the most spectacular combo shot, smooth as butter, and no one was here to see it! I only shoot no-slop, even when I'm practicing. At one point the cue ball was next to the five and it reminded me of an orange-sicle. Then the seven was next to the one, like ketchup & mustard, and I wanted a hot dog.

3.
Why do newscasters give away so many details of upcoming events when there is a security threat? "And over here you'll see what areas are blocked off, and they plan to have XYZ number of officers here and here." Geez. Why don't you hand out maps & timelines while you're at it!

4.
The newscaster had lapses in his synapses.

5.
I've seen enough commercials about menstruation.
Is that what you'd call a *period piece*?

6.
She dodged the Dodge, then dodged the dodge-ball.

7.
Watched movies with Blanca. Read a NY Times article Eve sent on how Ugandans move giraffes. Looked at a clip from my backyard camera over & over, trying to figure out if it was a cat or a raccoon that traipsed across my patio at 5:04am. Planted potatoes, weeded the garden. Zoomed with two friends. Left a delish beef stew out all night that I slaved over yesterday and I thought it was ruined, but three friends said it's still good because it's been so cold. Tried it and I'm still around to tell the story!

8.
THREE MORE DAYS!!!!!

9.
TWO MORE DAYS!!!!!

10.
TOMORROW'S THE DAY!

(Blanca & I still wish they'd move the ceremony inside for safety)

11.
A calm comes over me just seeing and listening to Joe and/or Kamala. Finally. Let's get the Cray-Cray-in-Chief out of there and bring sanity back.

END OF AN ERROR!!!

BIDEN & HARRIS ARE SWORN IN!!!
I cried through the whole thing, what a glorious day!

As Blanca & I leave you at the threshold of a new administration, we want to thank you SO MUCH for keeping us company during this crazy and history-making time.
You're the best.

Barb
XOXO

GIFT

A day so happy.
Fog lifted early, I worked in the garden.
Hummingbirds were stopping over honeysuckle flowers.
There was no thing on earth I wanted to possess.
I knew no one worth my envying him.
Whatever evil I had suffered, I forgot.
To think that once I was the same man did not embarrass me.
In my body I felt no pain.
When straightening up, I saw the blue sea and sails.

~ Czeslaw Milosz (1911-2004)

Going Down

© Eve Reynolds
2021
Ink and oil pastel on paper